INSTRUCTIONS

FOR

THE

LOVERS

DAWN LUNDY MARTIN

INSTRUCTIONS

FOR

THE

LOVERS

NIGHTBOAT BOOKS
NEW YORK

ISBN: 978-1-643-62231-6

Cover art: Detail from "Queen Mother" by Lyle Ashton Harris, 2019.
Copyright Lyle Ashton Harris. Reprinted with permission of the artist.

Cover design by Rissa Hochberger
Typesetting by Kit Schluter
Typeset in Plantin MT and Futura PT

Cataloging-in-publication data is available
from the Library of Congress

Nightboat Books
New York
www.nightboat.org

CONTENTS

After wind   was   water

After we were

water   when water

Subsumed   When the   thing

that was was

water   when   our   arms

were water   Our

gesture's flower   Our gestures   bloom

When it   was

                         When we   were when

water was not   When   we

subsumed
water

When   we   shivered

                    into

SERVICE

*But if her shining were not
for him, then who?*
—Toni Morrison, *Beloved*

THEN DEATH CAME LIKE
A HAMMER NOT A METAPHOR

As if to speak the body is to stroke the sack of it.
As if what remains will be comprehensible.

      We name it over and over, call
it into what would be being if being were
simply insistence. I want to believe in something.

I want to believe that effort is effect.

Meanwhile, a girl's head is crammed
      between her mother's knees,
the smell of her, the grease in her palms,
the pull of the girl's hair—tight tug into
      neat cornrows. Scalp archery. How many
people does it take to make a person?

I have had so many lovers, I forgot
      the one rape—me, a punishment
fusion. Float off down any stream, aimless
driftwood, the hollow of—the box contains
      me too.

The I feels nothing about it now, is
      gibberish to say, *to healing.*
We could say, instead, *we sand the hardened*—
like rip, like why even bother with refusal.

FROM WHICH THE THING IS MADE

In the end, I suppose, defeat is inevitable,
        the closing of something once delicately propped
open, a silk curtain floated back to its nature,
        or a mother, which is what this is really about—fetish of
the mother, the fetish of her under my tongue, bleating
        about. Even I can't let go, can't sift her being (that part
of her that's her) from my hands. What's wanted
        is not to be gotten, no frolic in dancing fields,
no cupping of the invisible cup, gentle water, soft hand,
        sweet ache of breath into mine. Mine, slats between—what
was it? What is it now? When your voice comes through
        my ear, technological and distant, the crack of it
as much a weapon as a frozen foot, as much the desert's
        reflective waterwell as any (   )—
You see that? My hands arching around what would be absence
        if absence were rot inside the body. We both hold it.

A forever flat road, nothing on either side, just air and land and
        fragrance like sun or metal—the I's sublime coma—
a road inside the throat to soothe the mother.

When I say absence, I say dirt under the grandma's
          fingernails, a break in speech like the drunken
cavern I enter each night to get outside of feeling, her
          name my name, her back, a nude trunk, rigid
in the face of—
Her God
a real God, in order to say, existence is not here under
          sabal palm, whatever dinosaur lingers in the unknown
body from nowhere. Records desist. Action truncation. I
          or, anyone can be the ur-unwitness, come sad
trinket of no remaining objects. When a person was, when
          the circumference was as narrow as a fly

what
          replaces them?

Speaking of replacements, of the way seeking never turns out
          quite right, and the animal in you grows a ratty teeth
substance akin to a quilt, really, your bare raw beat, a racket,
also, what holds you, what rips is also your own arms wrapped
around you, steady like blood, or the rivers that once were,
or flowers blooming after bombs and in the junkyard of the mind.

It's almost as if there's nothing outside of the experience of the body.
The repetition of the anapest seems necessary here—of the, of the,
ka clunk, "mind," "body," "experience"—this gap between all
ineffables and anything the I might say.

AS IF

As if the tender body is. As if the will is tender.

And, like any creature that has its hood up, you

take a photo of yourself in front of the window, rain

so dark, the day and vision desired, the way you are so

desperate for beautiful adventure the lights shut off

and the sweat of some hot stranger in your mouth. As if

to say *before* is to enter a house of filled with teenagers

piled on top of each other. Did I tell you that it's raining?

It's not hard to think that it's already night and necessary,

how any green is a wild form, and lastly, I don't want to

inspire devotion if it means the *I* becomes separated from the world.

Service as in swole as in undying, from the old
French, "act of homage, servitude, service at the
table," from the Latin, "slavery, condition of being a
slave," this blessing on knees, an opportunity of grunt
gratitude, thank you for this labor in my _____,
infinite waiting. Attentive in service, she said, to
gathering of _____ to fully _____ to steady
the body, uninterrupted.

THE INSTABILITY OF THE LOVER

To travel into and out of place [...] swift unnature of staying

becomes a frequency [...] you can no longer hear, the construct

of happiness, for example, how we long for a heartbeat.

Cement lot [...] willow tree, our bodies [before] beneath

splay, all sinew and glean, black drape and raw confidence. It's 1986

and freedom is something inevitable, the way brown boys run

shirtless, invisible siren roaring toward a fit mouth to bit it, O

from saying lightness, from—

What is the opposite of devastation? Fruit?

Family photo: the
unquenchable, the
cunt's expansive well.

PERSPECTIVE IS SUPPOSED
TO YIELD CLARITY

To waste years half alive, gumbled up in one's own lazy

wallowing, is how the tonic lay across me like a monster

blanket. I watched a lot of porn. I drank a lot of whiskey.

I let my body just wander around as if it had no mind, just

body and buzzing—the way vibration can make you hover

above yourself, and the feeling is exalted, and you don't ask

any questions at all about what life means. A bit of animal

is the secret to the unasked question, an openness to squander

what will cease to exist anyway. And, yet what quarantines do

not produce a desert of wifely longing? What kind of current,

what kind of system, what kind of wealth, what kind of birthright,

or digging, or commonwealth insistent on its own bright realm:

territories of defeat. And yet, the garden, swathed in bronze sunlight.

A bruise is a figure of remembrance, its blue eros hums.

"It was said that their relation made a generative

horizon line for all who were willing to look."

THE COMING THING

She said, I wish I prayed, I would pray for you. And,

we all wanted a shape of prayer in our brains, taking over

instead of it chomping on itself. Stupid little elf. God has

never come to me. We surrender in the teeming utterance

of materials soaked with sentences already made in air

and by machines. The country says Freedom, crushed under

its own dream weight. I did not make up this song. Design

Within Reach is having a "Work from home sale." The coming

apart, the giant laceration across the sky, we all feel it. Look

at the fire, look at it, like all the rage of all the smallest beings.

DIS-EASE STALKS THE LOVER

—humans

emerge from cement beams, flail out into sun,

hum emptiness like flies, and burdens, bottoms of shoes

all contaminated. Surfaces lie, steel distractions, distorted

visions, the reflection of one's face on a subway pole. I'm far

away from it, tucked in, writing from bed, blue sky, dead obligation

on my tongue. I can still taste it. Isn't that funny? Zurita burned

his face with a branding iron. When we itch, is what that says.

I

squint and see into—

not sure—all the things I'd thought I'd forgotten...

NO LANGUAGE
SUFFICES THE LOVER

Relief in not being stranded in a queue,

catching another human's skin fragrance, little invisible particles

of otherness entering the nose stream, their peculiar grief

of living.

      All around us decay. We can't smell it,

        the white mills,

white air between us.

Pretend we exist.

Try language, try excessive sweetness.

No names for things.

No names for phenomena.

Wound gathers around borders.

How long can we live without a body?

Once, the body, once its spiked desire.

Future Photo: As
we transform
this body horny
contentedness

BECAUSE

"Because" was a way of linking relations between occurrences,

to say the broken foot was accidental, for example. Reasons,

in addition to Reason, inert, dangled at the ghost mall.

The pattern of discipline no longer wears the face. Is simply

a way of organizing time, which was a fiction before,

now become edifice. Because we are a people, we used to say

structural diagramming was to determine a set of appropriate

movements for our comings and goings.

SILVER LAKE, FEBRUARY 2020

Elsewhere, corporeal men made to eat at each other's

necks. Hundreds upon hundreds—a caterpillar, iron in the face.

Think of other body-rows, other shit and piss baths. Think of

acquiescence. Now think of the stratosphere, of being slightly beyond.

I've been given a life to carry around and nurture its preciousness,

to say "me" and then to look out and see there's nowhere to

go. I remember the way California holds itself

distinguished in elemental cacophony. Things just glow. Even

there, a cotton wad filled my mouth, went all glut from

misuse. Hey, firestar, I used to say, come on over here

and let me walk you, and the answer was mostly, yes.

SENSE

"Sense," the first sacrifice—that cohesion dispersed. Only

lull left, "pause," they say, no such thing as "culmination"

unless cupping the squeezed-out life, black, a delicate furry thing.

Disturbances and gun buying. My mother refuses everything.

Her body is mostly skin, mostly enduring. I hear hope in her voice.

She tells me, when the pain ends, when calm comes, she's going

to buy me a birthday present and it's going to be a good one.

Remember? Soft to fingers, rain, the clean feel of snow?

The way a child body can walk through the blizzard unbeknownst to anyone, invisible and deep inside of her own feeling space. Somewhere else a cage rattles. In that place, fingers raw to bone. But, here, gorgeous desolation, and the first remembered sign of one's selfness. The I emerges, a staff, a kingdom.

what it has always been: a woman lounging on a velvet chaise or a woman doing someone else's laundry [figuration], a boy with a bag, etc. America cannot distinguish certain urgencies from faith. Drones overhead dumping something into someones. How to enter belief? [A quest] [A dissident reaction] I have said "everyone" but I've meant, "a few." I have said "chaos" but I meant "catastrophe." The whole nature of loving another person. I have said, "everything," but really, the poem is meant to register the particulars: these pants from Anthropologie like black balloons. There's a black man on my street walking with a bat and safety goggles, his little white poodle trailing behind him wearing a sweater. The first touch in a dark bar hallway, just the right pressure, a voluptuous sinking. Narrative, right out the window if there could be a window.

INSTRUCTIONS

FOR

THE

LOVERS

THE LOVER IN SERVICE TO /
IN SERVICE TO THE LOVER

"An expectation is repressed want. Repression makes a hardening of feeling. A list of what one seeks in love, a confusion between clarity of want and fixing a narrative."

A WILD WEED

Wild as in thunder, far off Catskills
sky strikes a dim hum so we say it as
it is said, "hold," "grounding," "pressure"
"pace, "not luck but tumbling, "buckling"
an earth that was once   intent on its own
              inner movement   unstroked   unmolested

That human intervention. Who knew?
That a weed could be a tree
before a scissor could be a cut
the strangeness of recompence
hearty in service   broken open kilter
An order deserves   maintenance

And yet, what savagery disrobes inside order?
What street fight made fragile in a hot
face glow parted so that, so that
all liquid is in retrieval.

When   want

becomes need

desert husk

INSTRUCTIONS FOR THE LOVERS

The lover was here and then was not. This is always the case. The lover persists in loverness and then, poof. Not poof poof but out of the kitchen and casual nakedness. The lover is a long tail though. Whipping around. Not understanding the sublime beauty of respite. I used to fuck almost any body out of starvation hunger that splits the one into many and leaves you arching toward a stinky mattress on a floor. It could be. I could have been. Times when the world dissolved into waves. Who knows that kind of blurry nothingness. Nothing is due. The more my father died the more mattresses. Floors and car interiors. Dirt. Dark air. Hallways. Un-destinations. Railway car junkie smelling of Eau Sauvage Dior.

"Lover" is incorrect to describe the lover. No English
word for the labors of ██████████

Opening, red fabric, legs wanting to be that. There is want and then there are stones. I was a stone once myself. A smooth blind projection. *I create you in the image of my desire. Which makes you nothing.* I forget my own desire, which has a blame factor. A record of convolution. Remember, L----, *I become consumed in waiting and then there's nothing else. All time is nothing. The days just pass and I'm in anguish.* Anguish is a red hurt, basalt. The time of expanded presence. What if we're all lovers. What if we're all little books. Little consequences.

The entanglement of loverness meant that when the world disappeared, we could not feel our subjugation. Cradled by the beloved. Enveloped, however temporarily, in the confines of bloom, the consumption of the ego. We swagger forth into our gendered selves alongside American rivers. My cap tilted sideways. Resolution stands like a remnant. Call forth the tatters of any lover correspondence and dip into its performance. *I'm not dying anymore*, you whisper into the lovers' ears. In the henceforth, what remains is tumbleweed lining the throat. It swells, heartbeat in ears disintegrates all knowledge. Dear lover, you know I lie.

Once I reclaimed the word "cunt" from a boy which is what he called me because I would not act like a girl should and the recklessness of that refusal until the boy sat on linoleum floor pile and me too upon sweet gestural violence, like you said, we're like this because of our trauma. That was years ago. Now, the I that inhabits this earth realm disagrees. Degrade me, it's okay. We're yearning for blood, for scar, any permanence.

I want a life of deep connection, I said to the lover. These things, why say them? I do not "have" this lover anymore possessed as I am by connection and loving. Want to have. Want to tuck away under my smelly arm pit. Want then to release into the world like a wounded bat I healed. I thought that lovers were a resemblance for my use, speaking of service. The day is long. Beautiful use is a lover who waits naked for hours self-bound. She called me "fragile" and then a "superhero."

Insert body turning to dust. Insert hollowed out brittle bone. Insert a body not sexed enough to be body. Bodying anyhow. The Domestic Sphere and its comforts—cradle rocking, kitchen clang, being fed in the mouth. Too much abundance, the economists tell us, leads to dearth. Turn your desire inward. (Eats a rock saw.) Turn light dial toward dusk. (Fire pit blaze pelvic floor.) Streeting habits   return J. Crew suiting flummoxed. Highbrow heat. Distinguished feather mouth mumbles _____.

ALL OF IT

Turning three times, by

    its nature, unprecipitous—a bar

where I did not long, the stripped

    dearth of the material world

naked. Elemental. Fire. A Cathedral

    where I did not belong

      or in lewdness

as if my cunt was dragged on its

    marble floors. To locate

oneself in place can be a horrible thing

    depending on the place

and the self. In this case, a straddling

    between worlds and, and

I am my own therapist, I said out

    loud, drunk with demotion

I'd built with intention on a front

    porch, my body

slathered in venom. A wild weed.

—

REPRESSED DREAMER

Protection
        was said, the dead space of
sleep—that parachuting down
        not fear, exactly, upon
descent or from where a consciousness
        emerges, eyes crusted shut.

—

How this world, too, is wet
        Staccato reach, an elsewhere,
a knowability from Hudson, New York
        wallow in a slow waiting
as if time were a mirror, as if to smother
        delight, always a grief howling,
if you choose to hear it, night eyes,
        if we choose to use them. It's
tuckered. Ravenous. Masked refugees
        clanging on. And, yet, on
        my own lips, wet like earth
        or an uncovered dream, just dripping
        echoic with a whole other night
        call. Like a welt. There is always
        here now, curled into a sofa,
        touch that is already touch, of
        beasts inside the chest, flagrant
        pull, the burn of it. They say, the sea grows,
        its reckless imagination, a prickling like skin.

ABOUT ART, D + D

We must make language of all forms of art together.
What art produces is a different language—untranslatable.

But then why want to ask questions when looking at art?
Language happens to be how we know ourselves to exist.

Or how we know we are unknowable.
I am not sure if art, produces.
Is it lonely then? Art?

It's both lonely, and a calling into the possibilities of shared.
Art can't ever be done.
Then it must produce. It makes babies.
Between the persons and the art I'm saying is something other
made possible by that interaction between persons and art.

For so many reasons I wish I could have seen these works with you.
Yes, to me art is, relationships.
I think we're saying something different this time.

Tell me.
Another way toward this is that art casts a spell. Not on no one.
And material or substance is produced inside of the interaction.
The engagement makes. Even if it is one solo soul staring upon
and feeling.
Suddenly the artwork is not lonely. It's a mother.

And when the artist is making?
I rarely think about that.

I know.
THE ARTIST.

But is the artwork lonely here?
No because it is uneasy in becoming. Maybe this unease approximates pain.

NOTES

IN

RELATION

WINTER

No matter
    what
happens, however
    tragic or who
says what with
    whatever kindness
or malice or whatever
    is done in
the name of some
    imagined ideal
or whoever is
    on their knees
groveling for mercy
    No matter which
open palm is raised
    a common gesture
and the fury
    of it all to
create a beautiful place he said
    amidst the easy
brutality of that like Fred said
    and like I said
it's a reminder
    not to put lead in
my feet as if
    the nation did
not simply yawn
    into its own

mouth trying to be
            itself
a tango
            a sweaty machine
impossible tether
            A whale decomposes
on the ocean floor
            didn't you know
the sea is a giant grave
            where else would they
go? My mother cannot tie
            her shoes' flat argument.
Does tyranny have its own
            music trying to find shape?

———

At the university, we
            exhausted a brand
of racism and wanted another
            wanted whatever was
wound by invisible wire
            our eyes blotted by stones
We could be fresh again
            eager bird minds lift
up our nasty bird throats
            a gully to soak sound
            trampling each other
            with envy.

———

—

"African Americans," they called us
                to shave the spikes off
our rage. I escaped to the long light
                of island time, a swollen
expanse like the breathing sea, amongst
                the grizzled Whites, who
could tell how old, skin
                a joyless confetti. Wherever
we were, the smother of their
                large bodies, monstrous
shadow would not shift
                its weird attachment.

You've heard about it
                Hands, clamorous forceps
quaffing rum and ale. We're all
                dying for a sea spray
into our nostrils, powder
                away the bureaucrat
endlessly twining toward
                nothing, the war,
the "standing with," all of it
                the other world, almost
fetish catastrophe. I swallowed
the seeds too. I left them inside me
to rot without a thought.

—

—

Because a way of getting
        got is split—wedge—
reduction to rudimentary tool-
        use or a slow killing
imperceptible, eye restrained
        floating in burial
dirt, my father adrift, weeds:

        Toward scythe, a swinging
        toward recompense
        what's held in that bubble between loss and—

        Black body as severed wing

It is winter
        grey cement has become
my face gazes into
        cracked accolades
bottomed out race labor
        a merciless hunt
behind me, a diving that looks
        like falling.

        —

—

Into my breath I breathe
        my dog's last breath
tell him it's okay
        like Alice said
absent weight of him is
        what I feel
that other world
        as dim and unjustified
as any closet filled with worms
        and to howl is the whole poem's
most corporeal flank
        when hit, a crippling.

SELF CARE

We, annihilated by rigor
   wet close to edges
of ornate buildings meant
   to keep us safe
they said safety was a priority
   no reason for coercion
grammar's meaning
   undisputed or so they
said in black and white
   It says right here
Tigers for populous! Take it
   or leave it
and holy water dripped from tongues
   unable to absorb
anything
   anymore
Meanwhile, outside the gates
   obsessive chatter about Freedom
which they said was
   doing whatever you want
whenever you want
   with whom or what
unintended or purposeful
   on land or sea or flying
The tower's upper window
   empty
irresistible lure
   ticked a lever in the chest for flying

What are the parts you don't remember?
Which evidence points toward exosphere?

So we lifted our one half-broken wing, and we flew
            we unsquatted, recalled
the medicinal qualities of the Boswellia tree.

ABOUT SECRETS, D + D

I like secrets though. I think about the way secrets are a product of a shared. Secrets are a necessary part of how people form, locate themselves and each other. *The secret is crucial for the erotic. And devastating for what happens after the moment of foreclosure.* If a secret is held right where the nature of the secret is shared and understood, the disclosures are less personalized, so the devastation is still present but shifts from altering truth to the multiplicity, ever present (loss) against oneness. *How can a secret be shared when the very word "secret" means apart?* The secret isn't shared, but the purpose of the secret is shared. *What if I, say, accidentally murdered your hamster, and that's the secret?* If you accidentally murdered my hamster, I would know you didn't tell me because you have your own feelings about it that you were processing before processing my reaction/response to it. *A secret is a promise in reverse. Which is the weapon? Which hurts the most? For example, it's just us on earth now and our eyes are quite dry. We think we hear a yodeling from afar. We reveal the door.*

INSISTENCE ON BEING

Precarity as a form of divination. Looking into each light form and breaking as old as the human body—its devasting fragility. Only the mother knew the sclerotic neck bone calling it a fat mole. The gumption of that slang revealed itself in a melancholic gaze. Comfort and ease of hospital gown. Paper clothing. I did not touch. I wondered about proximity as potential touch. My own fixation on narrowing the gendered body. I wanted the skin just right above the skeletal frame. We can call it: free movement in concert with conquest. The old ways.

We belabored our gentle being. Tongue, ancient para-
site, stroking its own floor. You can't stop yourself. You
could never stop anything. All beginning and motor.
All stiffening and coming. How does one not become
with finality? She said, Maybe I am a concrete subject,
final brush. We rub hormones on our chests and hope
for the best as if *Lord* is enough of a prayer. If only
fuchsia like the weather.

Having never lost—

As the father was ruin—*down from*—

he emerged, after, in unearthen form like himself unrealized. What is a

self if not untether? What are the bounds of flesh and bone, sinews take

no rest, called teeth, retch where things were once hockey puck slick on

ice, for every riding was ease into—

Having been accustomed to the kind of grief that—

One carries in one's own splitting. It's not dangerous like they think.

Freud's idea of sublimation twists an ordinary logic. If you like to torture,

you like to torture, sir. Becoming a surgeon ongoings what began. The

social seam is night pierced, where it finds its needed fissure, rapt attention.

Impending, inevitable, the mother at the rim of,

gazing inside the dug hole—

One's own clutching toward before—

Pottery because vessels—because a sewn language—

carrying, we think, the back is an injured raccoon, it

steams, confused. *Where do I go?* Historical anatomy.

Water-saturated organs, water outside (not enough now)—

Mother does not drink enough water—

They feed her milk—

Percussive throat throb left side—

It's all in your head, they tell me—

What I hear is my own short voice.

NOTHINGNESS

What is it to be saying? Force speech, rape speech. I have no subjectivity or light subjectivity. Speaking, defunct. Land mass floats. And the forests have been felled. And the antlers, snapped. Morphed lips, already sewn. Most of us are keen to mouth the word "beast." Or so much chatter static. I am not saying anything either, am waiting and breathing. My body is speaking. Expressing the thingness of the thing. It chats at me, motoring. In the taxi, a tree shaped purple fragrance floats across face.

—

To be a red
scratch or
red scotch,
depending on
your ████,
calculation
of the sublime, or
the sublime itself—

Memory fixed—
—and
then splatter.
My mother in
her pink kitchen
washes what
the garden
and its grey
chemicals produced.
Outside, the gate
ajar, the dog
run wild-ing. A thing
called *girl splay*,
or *wheat heart*.
We could draw
a chalk line there.

This is not conceptual. This is a poem. You are a poem. I am.

The hesitancy.
The undoingness.

More secrets: humiliation as release.

The men say, "I want to stretch you out," feel themselves big in this small corner of the world. How chivalrous, the ache of any obvious sliding down. What would the poem be without wings to block out the light?

THE PHOTOGRAPHS:
BLACK ALIVENESS

The manner and sensation of how we pay attention to our being constitute our being itself, as well as what our being is/becomes in the world. —Kevin Quashie

Black Aliveness as sane, wild, alert, infinite, and forever.
—Ronaldo V. Wilson

Study is always becoming practice.
—Zun Lee

No one weeps, a day's decolletage plunges us into what desire leaves in the wake of a radiant abyss, black light—oxymoron of our being—voluminous shape, any shade of blackness, body body. A rose pressed between teeth. This wild intercourse: stillness. I dive into the white frame, my hair alive with a young newness of becoming JD Lighting Jay Birthday Cake Candles 1982. Where are we now? How could we know anything else but this textured comforter, fingers trace its web-white cracks, its shadow stains from the wear of existence.

Now, you enter submissively, bowing to qualities of light velvet as skin, interiors transport, of a strobe light world, the word an imagined form of being, black pose, stray keys come about, smear of dissidence in Rolling Stones and hand gestures, no nation mask, glimpse gaze out, a counterpoint to Christina Sharpe's anti-black weather. Frame what cannot be captured, what cannot be contained in the tattered corners, scotch tape residue. What vestiges of waters remain untraceable when it's not you and nem, but me and nem. Could be roil. As in, we got a dog. How you exit the stage.

Mama's straight lean held by snow sky, knee deep in invisible whiteness. *The black cockatoo has the most power.* Me and nem, nem and me, Jay eating meat sticks, ain't that something? The coming into being with company under magnolia tree. Sing with me: distinctive sensation of one's own vernacular background. Say, no need for the word "freedom" to account for what this is. Say, "nest," say my anchor, my glory, my sister's arm draped around me. Worlds in that drape.

All myths dislodged and down your throat they go. Go on, row a boat. Kick some rocks in that pungent yearn for access. Roots of your tongues hangry in the juggernaut, in periphery. There are times for radical privacy. There are times when the night is wet, when the moon shows up like an apparition in reflective glare. Only they/we know that's Uncle So and So, bright as what would be touch.

Monique just knowing she is so damn fine against a red Beamer. Somebody's momma's purse like a weapon. Little crib babies not caring. Swift in swag. Hats. Those collars. White walled tires. Penchant for protection, arms woven into cloth, how we do, a sign, a signal singing, no strain at all. If a photo is music, so tenderly it hums. If there is a "freedom" place inside Sylvia Wynter's "near total alienation," feel it now. Hang your hat on your hanging hands. Where the sun don't shine, it obliterates. Supposition: fractal. My hirsute maker, my subjectitude. We are not strangers in this strange land.

This is when Vickie and them was here still in their night clothes. We all had that gold couch, we all went to war. Her name's a number in Anchorage, Alaska. Boarding the tour bus and to _____ with love. You simply cannot know a blackness undefined. No claim toward blackness made. If the photo is a long song it is not the blues. Instead, I'll be home soon so be sweet and be faithful. Hold that space for me.

In (joying) where they lent a lab art thing / a hallelujah
in the baptism bath / a labyrinth / laissez faire / lasso
/ a way into a way out / no coming fire / or fistula /
rather, the whole moons / only light / what flash allows
/ its flicker / rogue route epistemes / our bodies made
daydream / looking in the sunset age 6 / him posturing
around the tree / the hands—the hands so delicate /
hands in grace, folded, hands signs' signaling the / holy
holiday spirit / our real names / bedside table with pills
and tissue / breath that heaves, into a depth so black
we cannot reach it—

As if before
As if before time

*Of course, this is true as a
process of learning but
when I think about lovers
I think of flying.* Flying
with? Flying away?
Flying up? Flying out
of? Or into? I had a
dream where I could
fly. I kept amazing
myself but like a bat I
couldn't take off from
the ground, I had to
be high up, taking off
from the heights of a
roof. *For me the
wholeness of the lover is
akin to soaring through
space or the air. The
experience lifts the body
from its gravitational pull.
Sometimes there's too much
gravity. And the body just
sinks down into the earth.*
It sounds like your
emotional clitoris
wants to be
transported from the
mundane. *It's more than
the mundane. It's the
administrative maybe? The*

bureaucratic? It's not transported from, it's being into. I think of my senses as a pathway to the divine, and in the moments when the physical and the divine are present at the same time, it feels like a homecoming, a remembering of what it feels like to be alive. *Have you ever experienced this?* I experience it all the time with myself. With lovers it's easy to forget oneself. It takes a kind of reminder that the body isn't a thing or a look or a worker bee or even a pleasure machine. *The lover is a distraction from this?* No, the ideal lover is a collaborator in this, and offers the possibility of expanding even more into the physical-etheric bliss place,

grounding and
opening at the same
time. *The bombardment
of the limits of time, by
the way. The limits of
sovereignty or reign. That
one chooses. This idea you
purpose a collaboration.
Maybe the lover is simply
a collaborator. We don't
know what will be
produced in the artmaking
of loverness.* I used to be
full of holes looking
for other holes to
mirror my holes or
other things to fill my
holes, which were of
course unfillable. Now
the holes are portals
into the bliss of the
complicated human
experience, which is
physical and
nonphysical at the
same time. Do you feel
like you need the
lovers for something
you can't reach
yourself? *Everyone*

*inhabits the position of
lover in this imagining. I
expand. I leak out. The
fragmented body takes new
forms. We are exuberantly
awake inside of being
lovers.* But sometimes
we forget to be the
best lovers to
ourselves, don't you
think? *I do not think
lovers are savior. We open
a portal/portals.* If you
were the most ideal
lover to yourself, what
would you help
yourself open in and
for yourself? *I try to be
an ideal lover to myself.
The problem is that I'm
an industry unto my own
mind.* And if your
mind could be a lover
for your body, helping
the body be exactly
what it is, at all ages,
shining.

ACKNOWLEDGMENTS

To love and be loved, to have loved and been loved. With gratitude for the depths of these experiences that expand one's sense of being alive. With gratitude for the lovers who came into the opening and created shapes and shaped me. With gratitude for the opening.

In these pages there are words that emerged from text exchanges with Dana Bishop-Root. Thank you, Dana, for being in loving conversation with me, for the words whispered into my ear.

The closing poem, "D+S on Lovers," which is a kind of coda meant to be read as itself an opening, emerged from text messaging with Stephanie K. Hopkins while we were sitting next to each other getting pedicures. Thank you, Stephanie, for this loving life conversation, for words that would not exist if we were not us.

Thank you to the editors of the following publications where some of these poems, excerpts, or versions of these poems first appeared: The Academy of American Poets Poem-a-Day Series, *Brooklyn Poets*, *Gulf Coast*, *Interim: A Journal of Contemporary Poetry and Poetics*, *Lithub*, *The Slowdown Show*, and *There's a Revolution Outside, My Love*.

In addition, some poems or versions of poems were originally published in the collaborative chapbook with Toi Derricotte, *A Bruise is a Figure of Remembrance: Poems in Conversation and a Conversation*, published by

Slapering Hol Press. Huge thanks to Toi Derricotte for writing poems that prodded my imagination in new ways and to the Hudson Valley Writers Center. Much love and gratitude to artist Zun Lee and curator Sophie Hackett and their team at Art Gallery of Ontario for inviting me to be a part of *What Matters Most: Photographs of Black Life*. Versions of poems appeared in the exhibition book with the same title.

If it were not for my two teachers of poetry—Marilyn Nelson and Myung Mi Kim—this book would not be. It is here, perhaps, where what I learned from both comes together most pronouncedly. Thank you to Duriel E. Harris and Ronaldo V. Wilson for always pushing me out of my comfort zone, you beautiful black geniuses; to my writer's group—Nicole Callihan, Kristin Dombek, Stephanie K. Hopkins, and Ada Limón for your super smart listening and hilariousness; and to Ariana Reines and Justin Phillip Reed, your inspiration during the Covid-19 quarantine over the internets. I love all y'all.

Finally, much appreciation for Stephen Motika and Nightboat Books for welcoming me back home.

DAWN LUNDY MARTIN is an American poet and essayist. She is the author of four books of poems: *Good Stock Strange Blood*, winner of the 2019 Kingsley Tufts Award for Poetry; *Life in a Box is a Pretty Life*, which won the Lambda Literary Award for Lesbian Poetry; *DISCIPLINE, A Gathering of Matter / A Matter of Gathering*, and three limited edition chapbooks. Her nonfiction can be found in *n+1*, *The New Yorker*, *Plough-shares*, *The Believer*, and *The Best American Essays 2019* and *2021*. Martin was the first person to hold the Toi Derricotte Endowed Chair in English at the University of Pittsburgh where she co-founded and directed the Center for African American Poetry and Poetics. Currently she is working on memoir titled *When a Person Goes Missing*, forthcoming from Pantheon Books. She is Professor and Distinguished Writer in Residence at Bard College.

NIGHTBOAT BOOKS

Nightboat Books, a nonprofit organization, seeks to develop audiences for writers whose work resists convention and transcends boundaries. We publish books rich with poignancy, intelligence, and risk. Please visit nightboat.org to learn about our titles and how you can support our future publications.

The following individuals have supported the publication of this book. We thank them for their generosity and commitment to the mission of Nightboat Books:

Kazim Ali, Anonymous (8), Mary Armantrout, Jean C. Ballantyne, Thomas Ballantyne, Bill Bruns, John Cappetta, V. Shannon Clyne, Ulla Dydo Charitable Fund, Photios Giovanis, Amanda Greenberger, Vandana Khanna, Isaac Klausner, Shari Leinwand, Anne Marie Macari, Elizabeth Madans, Martha Melvoin, Caren Motika, Elizabeth Motika, The Leslie Scalapino - O Books Fund, Robin Shanus, Thomas Shardlow, Rebecca Shea, Ira Silverberg, Benjamin Taylor, David Wall, Jerrie Whitfield & Richard Motika, Arden Wohl, Issam Zineh

This book is made possible, in part, by grants from the New York City Department of Cultural Affairs in partnership with the City Council and the New York State Council on the Arts Literature Program.